# Central Texas DWI Charge?

## Useful Info Revealed That May Help Fight Your Charges

By David Volk,
Frank M. McElroy,
& Michael Volk

ISBN: 978-0-9894779-9-4

*Design and Published by:*
Speakeasy Marketing, Inc.
73-03 Bell Blvd#10
Oakland Gardens, N.Y. 11364

www.SpeakeasyMarketingInc.com

888-225-8594

# DEDICATIONS:

*David: To my wife Eliza and my son David Jr., because without them, I am nothing.*

*Frank: To my son Michael and wife Teresa for their unfailing faith and enthusiasm.*

*Michael: To my parents, Michael and Rosalina, and my brother and partner David for their continued unconditional support.*

# DISCLAIMER:

This publication is informational only. No legal advice is being given, and reading this material creates no attorney-client relationship. If you are facing legal issues, whether criminal or civil, seek professional legal counsel to have your questions answered.

**Volk & McElroy, LLP**
3003 NW Loop 410, Suite 100
San Antonio, TX 78230
Ph: (210) 377-1414
www.WinMyDWI.com

# Client Testimonials

*I would highly recommend David to represent you, he was always there supporting me and consistently on top of my case as if I was his only client. My DWI was not only erased from my record but all other charges were dismissed. I was treated like his family member. My sincere thanks to you, David*      **- A DWI Client**

..................................................................

*Michael and David Volk defended me in a DWI case. They were very instrumental in having my case dismissed. Without their legal representation I firmly believe that the dismissal would not have been possible.*
     **- Ismael (A DWI Client)**

..................................................................

*In 2010, I was arrested for a DWI. David Volk and Frank McElroy helped me navigate through a very difficult situation. Upon first meeting they reassured me they would do everything they could to clear my name. Ultimately, I was found not guilty by a jury which I believe would have not been possible without their legal expertise. There were many times I had questions pertaining to the case and they articulated clear and concise responses. I felt there was a genuine and sincere concern for my overall well-being. They helped make a very difficult situation tolerable. I am extremely well pleased well with the outcome of the case, and would recommend them to anyone going through a similar situation.*

     **– Nick (A DWI Client)**

# TABLE OF CONTENTS

## ATTORNEY INTRODUCTIONS

Volk and McElroy, LLP is law firm based in San Antonio, Texas. Our firm is made up of three attorneys David Volk, Frank McElroy, and Michael Volk *(pictured from right to left)*.

We have a mixed practice focusing on DWI defense, criminal defense, family law, patent law, and personal injury.

### Volk & McElroy Has Extensive Experience Handling DWI Cases

The majority of the criminal cases we handle are Driving While Intoxicated (DWI) cases. In Texas, you can be charged with DWI if you drive or operate a motor vehicle *while intoxicated* due to the introduction of alcohol, an illegal drug, a dangerous drug, or any combination thereof into the body. In Texas, "Intoxicated" means that you have lost the normal use of your mental or physical faculties or have a blood alcohol concentration of .08 or higher at the time of driving.

The "typical" DWI case usually begins with a police officer pulling someone over for a traffic violation such as speeding, swerving, or even something as serious as a traffic accident. DWI police officers usually will then "notice" that the driver has an odor of alcohol on their breath, bloodshot and watery eyes, and slurred speech. You are asked to step out of their car to perform field sobriety tests. You are now *a suspect* in a DWI investigation.

Normally, three roadside field sobriety tests are given: 1) The Horizontal Gaze Nystagmus test, 2) the Walk-and-Turn test, and 3) the One Leg Stand test.

The first test normally given is the Horizontal Gaze Nystagmus or HGN. During this "eye test", the police officer looks to see if your eyes show a pronounced involuntary jerking when waving a pen or light from side to side across your face.

The next sobriety test given is usually the Walk-and-Turn test where the suspect is told to walk a straight line taking 9 heel-to-toe steps, turn around in an unusual way, and return to the starting position taking 9 heel-to-toe steps.

The third test is the One Leg Stand Test where the suspect is asked to stand on one leg for 30 seconds in a very unnatural stance.

As the suspect is doing these tests, the police officer is keeping score, but never reveals the criteria used to score the performance. The suspect also does NOT get credit for doing something correctly. The suspect is not given to a practice run.

Just when you think you passed the 3 tests with flying colors, the police officer arrests you and takes you downtown where you either give a breath test or a blood test. Now you are being charged with a DWI. Upon being booked, you now have criminal records that available to the public.

*How did this happen? And what do I do now?* Well, you go get yourself a lawyer. And you need a damn good one because your career, your record, and your reputation are on the line.

We have defended civilians and police officers charged with DWI and, on the other end of the spectrum, we have sued drunk drivers who hurt our clients in DWI-related car crashes.

We are advocates, and we advocate based on our client's needs. We are lawyers, plain and simple. That is what we do.

## Volk & McElroy Has Been Working with DWI Cases for the Past Eight Years, with Twenty Four Years of Combined Courtroom Experience

We are often asked about the number of cases we have handled over the years.

As of 2014, we have been doing DWI defense work for the last eight years. Between the three of us, we have defended hundreds of cases. Our lawyers have handled everything from a DWI misdemeanor to a enhanced DWI felony.

## Case Histories from Volk & McElroy

Our favorite recent victory in a DWI trial involved a young man whose job was everything to him.

## Because Everyone Deserves a Second Chance, Volk & McElroy Goes to Great Lengths to Advocate for Their Clients

We defended the director of a non-profit organization in San Antonio who was responsible for obtaining assistance for low-income families.

The client was in his 20s. His job was his entire life. He had no children and was not married. The Board of Directors at his nonprofit warned him, "If you do not beat the case, you will be fired. Immediately upon conviction you'll be terminated."

His case involved three experienced police officers from the San Antonio Police Department. Everything was captured on video. The first obstacle we had to overcome was the fact that he confessed on video that he had "f$%ed up really bad."

This victory sticks out in our mind because the lead officer, who was probably one of the most trained SAPD policemen, kept laughing at David Volk when he would make legal objections. David's first question to the policeman was, *"What's so funny? Is doing my job that funny to you?"*

After attacking the policeman's credibility on the witness stand and having our client give honest, sincere testimony, the jury found him NOT GUILTY.

Our client kept his job and got a second chance. Wins like this drive our passion for DWI defense.

## How It Is Possible to Prevail In Difficult Cases?

Exercising your right to a jury trial and attacking the admissibility of evidence before trial are some ways to win difficult cases. One of the most extreme cases we have tried to verdict resulted in a hung jury.

### Hung Jury

Our client was arrested and had his blood drawn after the police obtained a search warrant. The laboratory reported his blood alcohol as 0.20 grams of alcohol per liter of blood. That is nearly three times over the legal limit of 0.08 grams of alcohol per liter of blood.

When this case was called for trial in 2012, it became one of the first blood-draw misdemeanor

DWI cases tried in Bexar County after the District Attorney's no refusal campaign was instituted. Frank McElroy cross-examined the registered nurse who drew our client's blood and got her to admit on the witness stand that she did not know the definition of hemolysis (*i.e.,* process by which red blood cells rupture and release their contents into the surrounding fluid). He also got her to admit that the materials used to make up the blood draw kits were stored and put together in the District Attorney's Office. The analyst who tested the blood using a gas chromatograph admitted on cross examination that the blood was stored in a mini-fridge in the back of the booking area for several days before being transported to her office where it sat in another fridge for *several weeks* before it was tested along with over 100 samples from other cases.

Two of the six jurors voted not guilty because they did not trust the accuracy of the blood test even though the analysis put our client almost three times over the legal limit. The Court declared a mistrial due to a hung jury because the State could not get a unanimous guilty verdict from the 6 jurors. We avoided the conviction for our client that day even though the State was able to produce all the necessary witnesses to admit the blood test into evidence. When the case was recalled for trial several months later, the client accepted a plea to a lesser charge.

## Problems with the Prosecution's Case Can Lead to a Dismissal

We recently obtained a dismissal for a client with a 0.295 breath test.  We showed up for trial only to have the case dismissed the following day. The witness who was going to testify he saw our client driving had committed suicide a few weeks earlier, but the State did not tell us that until after the case was dismissed. Our client won his freedom simply by exercising his right to a jury trial and choosing to fight the case at all costs. Sometimes that is all it takes. If he had pled guilty during the pre-trial phase months earlier, he would have never known about the witness' death and would have the conviction for DWI on his record forever.

## In Volk & McElroy's Experience, It Can Be Possible to Prevail in a DWI Case, Even with High Breath or Blood Test Results

Having a high breath or blood test result does not mean you cannot win your case.

### THINKING ABOUT PLEADING GUILTY? DON'T DECIDE FOR YOURSELF WHAT THE OUTCOME OF YOUR DWI CASE WILL BE BEFORE CONSULTING AN EXPERIENCED DWI ATTORNEY

You may ask yourself after a DWI arrest, "Look, I drank. I was drunk. I'm guilty. Should I just give up?"

These people want to know what plea bargain options are available. They have already decided for themselves how the case will go, even though they do not have any knowledge of DWI. Sometimes family members or friends try to counsel them on what will happen, even though they have no legal experience of any kind.

When we interview new clients, we ask ourselves, "How difficult is it going to be for the State to prove this case?" Sometimes, the more outrageous the facts are, the harder it is for the State to present the case in Court.

For example, if 11 police officers were all on the scene of a DWI and all contributed to the arrest in some way, the prosecutor may have a very difficult time lining up each of those witnesses for trial. This is especially true when the jury trial date is a year or more after the arrest.

Good DWI defense lawyers go through the case step-by-step with the client before making any predictions about the outcome.

Here are some of the steps we take to prepare for Court: First, we check to see if the initial traffic stop was legal. If the stop was made illegally or without *reasonable suspicion*, any evidence from the DWI stop and arrest should be thrown out of Court. For example, weaving within one's lane is not a traffic violation under most circumstances and does not constitute reasonable suspicion for a stop.

Second, we investigate whether or not the police officer had *probable cause* to make a DWI arrest.

Third, we make sure the police did not *coerce* you into giving a breath or blood test. Next, we try to verify whether the breath or blood was taken and tested accurately.

### While Not Every Case Can Be Won, It Is Possible to Create a Viable Defense for Every Case

Not every case can be won, but a good DWI defense attorney can put together a valid, reasonable defense for any case.

People should never assume they are doomed, even if the case seems to be completely hopeless.

### YOU SHOULD ALWAYS CONSIDER RETAINING AN ATTORNEY TO DEFEND A DWI CASE; THE RIGHT ATTORNEY HAS THE NECESSARY TOOLS TO PREVAIL IN EVEN THE MOST DIFFICULT CASES

In some cases, the State has to throw in the towel and dismiss the case because there is something wrong with the police officer's credibility.

We were hired by a Federal Agent who was arrested for a DWI with a breath test of 0.10. He was adamant that the officer had lied about critical facts in the police report. There was no video of the arrest to corroborate our client's story.

We found out that the arresting officer had previously been disciplined for falsifying DWI reports by claiming he had given field sobriety tests when he actually had not. Another officer had reported him to internal affairs.

Good DWI defense attorneys will get copies of an arresting officer's disciplinary file before trial. For our client's case, this information was deeply hidden, but we were able to find it. Once we notified the District Attorney of this information, the case was dismissed because the police officer was an unreliable witness.

## IS AN APPOINTED PUBLIC DEFENDER OR SELF-REPRESENTATION A VIABLE OPTION FOR A DWI CASE?

Some people wonder if they should get a public defender or defend themselves after being arrested for DWI.

## Volk & McElroy, LLP Always Discusses All Available Options with Each of Our Clients

This is a discussion we have with each client whether they ask the question or not. There are costs associated with retaining an attorney, and the cost is something each client must consider. People do not plan on being arrested, so they do not usually have money set aside for legal representation.

## The Texas Courts Usually Discourage Self-Representation

Texas Courts usually discourage representing yourself at trial. First, it is virtually impossible for someone who is not an experienced attorney to know what factors to consider to build a DWI defense. Second, a person without legal experience will not likely be fully informed of their rights or the collateral consequences of being convicted of a DWI. Third, a *pro se* defendant (a non-lawyer who represents him or herself) without an attorney is held to the same standard as a competent, licensed attorney when it comes to Court procedures.

It is important to know that the Court and prosecutor cannot give legal advice to a person who is representing him or herself at trial. This is true even in small counties where a person may know the judge and prosecutor personally. Self-representation in a DWI case is a bad idea.

### The San Antonio Area Offers Court-Appointed Private Attorneys for Individuals with Limited Financial Means

San Antonio does not have a public defender system at the trial level. Public defenders are only available for appellate cases. Instead, the Courts maintain a list of private attorneys who agree to provide legal services as court-appointed attorneys and the attorney is compensated by the County.

### The Court-Appointed Attorney Cannot Represent You at the Administrative License Revocation Hearing Unless You Pay Them to Do So

Unfortunately, when a Court appoints an attorney for you, you do not get to choose the attorney you want. Court-appointed lawyers are tremendously

underpaid and cannot provide additional assistance
– such as representation at the Administrative
License Revocation Hearing or obtaining an
occupational driver's license for you - unless you
pay them to do so. This means that you may only
get a partial defense. As retained attorneys, we at
Volk & McElroy handle the additional legal issues a
person might face as a result of a DWI charge. We
bundle the driver's license representation as well as
assisting you to obtain an occupational license, if
needed, as part of our overall fee. Most DWI
attorneys who are retained will offer, or should
offer, these additional services when representing
you on a DWI. Whether you have an appointed or
retained attorney, you will be paying extra for these
additional services.

### Lack of Resources: The Court-Appointed Attorney Does Not Have as Many Available Tools to Build a Defense as Do Privately Retained Attorneys

Bexar County does not reimburse court-appointed
attorneys for many of the expenses a client would
need to successfully fight a DWI case. For example,
the County would not reimburse a court appointed-

attorney for obtaining transcripts of previous testimony from a driver's license hearing that can be helpful in building a successful defense.

Another problem is the huge variation in experience among court-appointed attorneys. Some court-appointed attorneys are very experienced, while others literally just got their license to practice law.

We recommend that when charged with a crime, make sure the lawyer you choose is the one you want *sitting next to you at trial*. Sometimes you get a great attorney with the court-appointed system; sometimes you do not. The same can be said for retained attorneys. Just because you pay someone does not automatically make him or her a brilliant attorney. It is important to have confidence in your attorney and that you select someone you trust.

### Volk & McElroy, LLP Advises Potential Clients to Allow Time to Interview Potential Private Attorneys before Deciding to Hire One

We always encourage people, whether they go the appointed attorney route or the retained attorney route, to interview the lawyer carefully and ask them about their experience in these types of cases. Ultimately, experience is what matters.

## DWI Defense Is an Area of the Law Where Experience Counts

Experienced attorneys will not be caught off guard as easily as an inexperienced attorney. If the lawyer has not dealt with specific issues in the courtroom that may come up during trial, he or she may be blindsided.

We have witnessed inexperienced lawyers try DWI cases and get caught off guard. Inexperienced attorneys will often agree with the prosecutor on certain issues without challenging them in order not to appear misinformed.

### Volk & McElroy, LLP are Experienced Trial Attorneys

The bottom line is that trial experience is what gives a lawyer an edge. The attorneys at Volk & McElroy also maintain extensive Continued Legal Education training and attend seminars nationwide on cutting-edge issues in DWI defense.

# BUILDING A DWI DEFENSE

Potential clients often want to know whether they should document what happened when they were arrested, or whether the attorney will go over the details with them during the consultation.

At Volk & McElroy, we typically have two types of clients: those who remember everything that happened and those who do not remember anything. The first thing we do is document as much information as they can remember during the intake process.

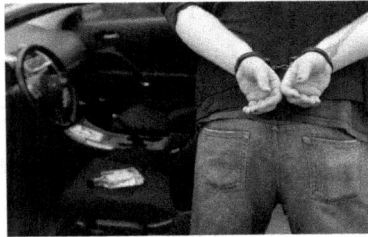

## While Having a Video Recording Is Beneficial, Volk & McElroy Asks Each Client about Their Interaction with the Police

We make every effort to obtain a video recording of our client'sarrest of it exists. Videos are helpful throughout preparation and trial. Our clients often provide interesting information about events that happened before and after the video was recording.

The police officer may make helpful statements that were not recorded on video. We recently handled a case in which the police officer shut off the video and then told the client, "Hey, you can probably beat this case if you get a good lawyer." Statements like this are game-changers even though it was not captured on video.

Using the client intake, the video of the arrest, the police report, and our communications with the client, we try to reconstruct what happened and come up with the best possible defense.

### Volk & McElroy, LLP Finds It Helpful to Visit the Scene of the Arrest

We like to visit the scene of a DWI arrest to see the lay of the land. We also use satellite images of the scene to see where the arrest happened. This is incredibly helpful in cases where the roadway is sloped, curved, or cracked to argue that the sobriety tests were done on an improper surface.

## WHAT TO AVOID IF YOU HAVE BEEN ARRESTED FOR DWI IN TEXAS

There are several common mistakes people make when they have been arrested that can sabotage their case. We have come up with three rules to make sure that our clients do not unintentionally damage their defense.

## Never Miss Your Court Appearance

First, go to court. Always make sure you are at your court dates. This is important because if you do not show up the Judge will issue a warrant for your arrest.

## Avoid Getting Re-Arrested

Second, do not get re-arrested. This seems easy enough, but we have clients who are arrested three or four subsequent times for other DWIs or other crimes *while we are representing them on their first DWI*. Not only does a re-arrest put you in a bad light with the Court, but you will also spend a whole lot more money to keep yourself out of jail.

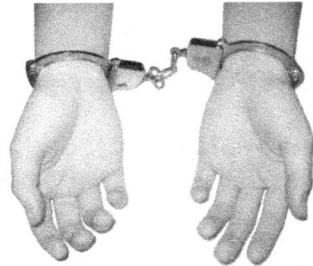

## Comply with the Conditions of Your Release

Finally, make sure you comply with the conditions of your initial release from jail. Sometimes the Court will require you to have ignition interlock on your vehicle. You must comply with that Court order. Blowing alcohol into that machine will cause the Court to take notice, and it will negatively affect your case.

Those are the three rules we tell our clients to follow. If the client follows these three rules, we can focus our attention on fighting the charges rather than keeping our client out of jail for post-arrest behavior.

## COMMON MISCONCEPTIONS ABOUT A DWI CASE

There are several common misconceptions prospective clients make about DWI cases.

### It Is a Mistake to Assume You Will Receive Leniency for a First Offense

The first misconception is that people assume that because they have never been in trouble before their case will automatically be dismissed. This is not true! In fact, we have seen the State prosecute the case more aggressively if the defendant is a police officer, attorney, a doctor, or

somebody in a professional position with a lot to lose.

People sometimes ask, "Look, it's my first time being in trouble. Can't you just ask to the Judge to dismiss my case? I've never been in trouble before, and I have a great job. They will fire me if I get convicted. Can't I just pay a fine and have it taken off my record for good?" DWI is a crime that can happen to anybody. People do not intend to break the law when they have that first drink. The reality is that you cannot buy your way out of a DWI case. The Courts and law are very tough, even on first time offenders.

## A DWI Conviction in Texas Cannot Be Expunged from Your Record

An expunction is a legal process in which criminal records are destroyed when a case is dismissed, dropped, never charged, or acquitted by a jury. People often misunderstand how an expunction works. They sometimes believe that if they are on probation for DWI it can somehow be removed or expunged from their record in the future. This is simply not true.

If you are convicted for DWI, that conviction stays on your record for the rest of your life.

## Because of Escalating Penalties for Subsequent DWI Convictions, It Is a Mistake Not to Fight a First Offense DWI

People often believe that they should not fight a first DWI charge and that they should just plead guilty. However, this can set you up for a lot more trouble later on.

We are hired to defend as many DWI 2nd offenses as DWI 1st offenses. Clients on their second offense usually tell us that on their first DWI they spent little time choosing their lawyer, went to one Court appearance, and hastily took a plea bargain for probation.

### In Texas, a Second DWI Entails a 30-Day Jail Sentence

DWI penalties escalate with subsequent convictions. A second DWI entails a 30-day jail sentence, even if the client previously completed probation for a first DWI. The 30-day jail sentence is an enhanced sentence that would not be on the table if the client had beaten their first DWI case.

Assuming that you should not fight a DWI 1$^{st}$ is a common mistake. People often say, "I was arrested when I was younger. I just took care of it and got probation, and I did not really fight it." You should be aware of the consequences of not fighting your first DWI, should you get arrested again.

## WILL A DWI CHARGE BE PUBLIC KNOWLEDGE?

Clients worry about the publicity of their DWI arrest and whether their employer, co-workers, friends, or family can find out.

### In the San Antonio Area, the Record of a DWI Arrest Is Easily Accessible Online

This is a very common concern. When a person is arrested for DWI, the arrest immediately becomes a matter of public record. If you know where to look online, anyone can pull up information about the arrest. This includes the date of arrest, the arrestee's jail identification number, the court in which the case is set, and when the next court date is scheduled.

While Bexar County publishes all of this information online, the County Courts will not call a person's work and report the arrest. If a workplace does routine background checks, the information surrounding an arrest is easy to find and will likely pop up.

## The Information about Your Arrest Is Available Even If You Are Acquitted or Your Case Is Dismissed

While the case is pending, and even if it is eventually dismissed, the information about your arrest is available online. Your employer can find it. Your friends and family can find it. They just need to know where to look – and the information is easy to find.

In some cases, a simple Google search of a person's name will display their mugshot. The picture can show up on a mugshot database website within a day or two after the arrest. Unfortunately, this is very damaging to clients because they are publicly branded a criminal before they have even had a court date.

These websites also make it difficult to explain to people that they are presumed innocent while the case is pending.

# In the San Antonio Area, There Easily Can Be More Than 100 DWI Arrests a Week

If you are arrested for DWI, you are not alone. Sometimes more than 100 people are arrested in a week for DWI in Bexar County. This number is particularly possible on holiday weekends.

DWIs are newsworthy in San Antonio because they happen so frequently. We have defended clients whose DWI cases were publicized by the news stations.

## The San Antonio Area Has a High Volume of Wrong-Way Drivers Also Charged with DWI

San Antonio seems to have an epidemic of wrong-way drivers. There have been at least 10 or 15 wrong-way driving DWI cases in the media where people were injured or killed, including police officers.

# DWI FACT OR FICTION: CAN YOU EXPECT TO RECEIVE MERCY FROM THE COURT?

People often use the expression "what if I put myself at the mercy of the Court. "

If a jury has found a person guilty, they will have to put themselves at the mercy of the Court because the Judge will determine the person's sentence (if they have elected to go to the Judge for punishment rather than the jury).

## You Should Present Yourself in the Best Possible Light to the Judge Hearing Your DWI Case

While your case is pending, during trial, and after the verdict, you want to present yourself in the most favorable light to that Judge. Doing so may help minimize any punishment assessed.

## Being Proactive: Volk & McElroy Will Advise You Accordingly

We recommend that our clients are proactive while their cases are pending. We encourage our clients to take proactive measures by doing things such as community service and/or alcohol counseling/treatment if the client feels they need to do so. By following our advice, they will be able to show the Court they did not waste the Judge's time with the jury trial, that there were defendable issues in the case, and that you are accepting the jury's verdict with humility and remorse. They are also addressing proactively any alcohol dependency so that they avoid a second arrest.

## DURING A DWI ARREST, IS A BREATH TEST OR BLOOD TEST MORE COMMONLY ADMINISTERED IN THE SAN ANTONIO AREA?

Every person arrested for DWI in Texas is asked to submit to a breath or blood test. Once the officer feels he or she has *probable cause* to arrest you for DWI, he or she will read you a document called the *DIC-24*. This document advises you of the statutory consequences of refusing to voluntarily submit to a breath or blood test.

## Blood Draws with Warrants Have Been Recently Instituted to Combat the High Incidence of Breath Test Refusals

In 2012, Bexar County magistrate judges started issuing search warrants for forcible blood draws. Before this policy went into effect, many arrested for DWI refused to give a breath test.

Under the current policy, if a person refuses a breath test in Bexar County, the officer will apply for a search warrant to the sitting magistrate Judge. Once signed, the warrant is typically executed by having an in-house nurse draw the client's blood just outside their holding cell. If you do not cooperate with the nurse, the police will strap you down to a chair and forcibly take your blood.

We are still handling a few older cases in which there is no breath test or blood test. Blood draw trials are relatively new in San Antonio but are becoming more common.

### In Volk & McElroy's Opinion, Blood Tests Can Be As Defensible Than Breath Tests

People think blood testing is more accurate than breath testing; however, there are many factors that can make a blood draw DWI case as defendable as a breath test.

First, Bexar County prosecutors are not as experienced trying blood draw cases. Second, when someone's blood is taken in Bexar County, the period of time before it is actually tested can be quite lengthy. Typically 1 to 4 weeks can pass before the blood is tested. We have found that this bothers jurors immensely because they would prefer that the laboratory test the blood right away.

### Volk & McElroy Finds That Some Jurors Disapprove of the Way the Blood Sample Is Handled

Blood samples often sit in a refrigerator in the back of the magistrate's office for a couple of days before the Bexar County medical examiner or some third party laboratory hired by the District Attorney's Office receives it. Several more weeks may pass before the blood is tested. We have found that some jurors do not like this.

Whether breath or blood, the attorneys at Volk & McElroy are prepared to fight both types of cases. Experienced defense lawyers have litigated both types. Make sure when you hire an attorney you ask if they have tried breath and blood cases in front of juries.

## No More Refusals: The Blood Draw Policy Is Now Mandatory

The days of total refusal cases, in Bexar County at least, are over. Some of the surrounding counties may file DWI charges without a breath or blood test.

## Volk & McElroy, LLP Recently Had a Favorable Outcome in a Case Where a Blood Draw was Possible but was Not Administered

Recently we had a client who was alleged to have clipped his neighbor's car at a gas station, fled the scene, and crashed into a ditch outside of Hays County. When police arrived, he admitted to consuming large amounts of alcohol and Xanax. He refused to provide a voluntary sample of his breath or blood. Upon his arrest, the police did not seek a search warrant to forcibly take his blood. The police felt their evidence was so strong against him that they did not need the blood test. Unfortunately for the State, the officer who arrested him was moonlighting as a security guard at the same time he was on patrol, so he was literally receiving two paychecks while arresting our client. Due to the police officer's dishonesty, we were able to resolve that case in our client's favor despite the aggravating circumstances. Our client was not convicted of DWI. He received unsupervised deferred adjudication probation on a much lesser charge. He was able to save his career and will be able to seal the reduced charge through a legal process called a nondisclosure of criminal records.

## WHAT FACTORS CAN RESULT IN AGGRAVATED DWI CHARGES?

Some of our clients at Volk & McElroy are charged with aggravated or enhanced DWIs.

### High Blood Alcohol Levels Can Result in Enhanced Penalties

A DWI 1st in Texas is a class-B misdemeanor. The legislature recently changed the law so that if your blood alcohol is alleged to be a 0.15 or higher, the case is enhanced from a class-B misdemeanor to a class-A misdemeanor. This enhanced charge is called DWI with a BAC of 0.15 or higher.

Penalties associated with a class-B misdemeanor range up to $2,000 and 180 days in jail, whereas the enhanced charge of BAC with a 0.15 or higher can be up to a $4,000 fine and up to 365 days in the county jail.

If you are charged with a DWI 1st and have an open container of alcohol in the vehicle, there is a requirement of 6 days mandatory jail time as a condition of probation upon conviction.

## A Third DWI Offense Can Be Charged as a Felony in Texas

A DWI 3rd or more is a third-degree felony. You must have previously been convicted of at least 2 DWIs in the past to be charged with a felony DWI. A third degree felony is punishable by up to a $10,000 fine and 2 years to 10 years in the Texas Department of Corrections.

## Having Children in the Car While Intoxicated Is a Felony Charge

Having children in the car during a DWI is a state jail felony. A state jail felony is punishable by up to a $10,000 fine and 6 months to 2 years in the state jail prison.

## Causing an Accident with Serious Bodily Injury Is a Charge of Intoxication Assault and a Felony

If someone is seriously injured as a result of a DWI related car crash, the driver can be charged with intoxication assault – a third-degree felony (carries the same range of punishment as a DWI felony even if the client has no prior record). If a person is killed because of that accident, the driver can be charged with intoxication manslaughter. Intoxication manslaughter is a 2nd degree felony punishable by up to a $10,000.00 fine and 2 to 20 years in the Texas Department of Corrections.

# YOUR DRIVER'S LICENSE AND A DWI IN TEXAS

Many clients are concerned about what happens to their driver's license after they are arrested.

## The Status of Your Driver's License Depends on Your History and the Facts of the Case

Driver's licenses revocations are handled on a case-by-case basis. Suspension periods and reinstatement of a driver's license depends on the client's age, driving record, and outcome of the Administrative License Revocation Hearing.

Generally speaking, if you consent to a breath or blood test and the result is above a 0.08 on your first DWI, then your license will be suspended for 90 days.

If you refuse a breath test (even if they get your blood with a warrant), your license will be suspended for 180 days.

## It Is Advisable to Consult with an Attorney to Learn about the Potential Consequences to Your Driver's License

We encourage people who are facing a DWI to make sure that your lawyer carefully looks at your driving history and arrest record to predict how long your license may be suspended after a DWI arrest.

**You Can Fight Your Driver's License Suspension But Must Request the Hearing Within 15 Days of Your Arrest or Else it is Waived**

Most DWI attorneys offer the service of representation in the Administrative License Revocation Hearing, or ALR hearing. You or your attorney must request that hearing within 15 days of your arrest. Once the hearing is requested, that will put any potential driver's license suspension on hold. If your attorney wins the hearing, your license will not be suspended.

## DOES TEXAS ALLOW OCCUPATIONAL LICENSES?

Many people are not aware that they might be eligible for an occupational license.

For a first-time DWI license suspension as a result of administrative license revocation (ALR) hearing, we can help you obtain an occupational license. The type of Texas driver's license you have at the time of your arrest will determine the type of liberties you will have with an occupational license.

**Volk & McElroy Has Been Able to Obtain Occupational Licenses for Clients Facing a Second DWI Offense**

If the offense is a second DWI, or more, you still can obtain an occupational license. The process is a bit more complicated because you have to have a hearing set and notify certain agencies.

An occupational license is useful for people because it allows them to travel to school and work. It may also be used to drive for essential household duties such as doctor visits, going to the grocery store, taking kids to school, or even going to church.

## DWI AND COMMERCIAL DRIVERS

Our attorneys are experienced in handling DWI cases for drivers that hold a Class A commercial driver's license. These individuals rely on their CDL for their livelihood for 18 wheeler driving, bus driving, or even commercial auto/truck sales.

### A CDL Holder Must Maintain a Clear Driving Record

A DWI conviction has major consequences for a CDL driver.

If you have a CDL and are convicted of a DWI, or if your license is suspended because of the ALR hearing, your privilege to drive your commercial motor vehicle will also be suspended. Even if you obtain an occupational driver's license, you will not be allowed to drive a commercial vehicle. The law does not make exceptions even if you stand to lose your job and sole means of income for your family.

## It Is Advisable for a Commercial Driver to Retain an Attorney for Any Alcohol-Related Offense

There are additional consequences you may face if you have a commercial driver's license. We encourage anyone who holds a CDL to hire a competent attorney to handle their DWI.

## UNDERAGE DRIVERS AND A DWI

Many of the DWI cases we have handled at Volk & McElroy involve underage drivers.

## Drivers under the Age of 21 Face an Additional License Suspension for a DWI Conviction

If you are under 21 and are convicted, you face not only the initial ALR suspension but also an additional license suspension upon conviction. The suspension ranges from 90 days to one year upon conviction. The State of Texas sends a message that they will give underage drivers a harsher penalty than adults. The underage driver should not have been drinking at all, and certainly not to the point of becoming intoxicated.

We encourage underage drivers to fight their DWI because we do not want them to lose their license a second time.

## DRUG-RELATED DWIS

DWIs most commonly involve alcohol, but can also involve drugs, both illegal and/or prescription drugs.

## Many Drivers Are Unaware of the Penalties for a Drug-Related DWI

One of the most common misconceptions is that people believe they cannot be charged with DWIs unless they have been drinking alcohol. A person can be charged with DWI if they have consumed an intoxicating combination of drugs and alcohol or drugs alone, regardless of whether the drug is a prescription medication or an illegal drug.

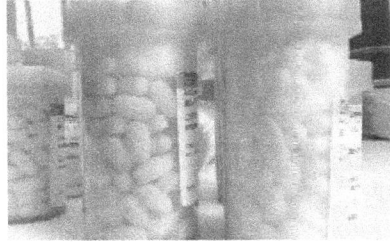

## Gauging the Level of Drug That Causes Intoxication Is Difficult

One difficult part about defending drug DWI cases is that prosecutors are typically not as familiar with what levels of toxicity of certain drugs cause intoxication. People who take prescription medication develop a tolerance to it. The prosecutors will not spend time getting to know the defendant's medical history or trying to understand how the drugs affected them while driving. They will simply get a lab report that has a reading on it for a certain drug, or metabolite of a certain drug, and not give consideration to the person's medical history. It is not so easy for DWI defense attorneys either. It takes a combination of knowing your client's medical history regarding the prescription as well as some knowledge in the field of toxicology.

### Drug-Related DWI Defense Requires Some Expertise on the Part of the Defense Attorney

Often DWI attorneys will employ their own experts to explain the following simple fact: If someone is taking a prescription medication, they are directed to take that prescription because they *need* it to feel normal.

If someone has had a major back injury, back pain is the ultimate distractor. That patient should take their prescribed dosage of medication to attempt to stabilize their pain. Problems arise when a prosecutor looks at the test results and believes that the person was driving during a drug binge. Our job is to explain to the jury why the person had that level of prescription drugs in their system. Many clients cannot afford experts in their case, and the DWI defense attorney must attempt to pull that information from cross-examination of the State's toxicologist.

**Currently, Texas Does Not Have a Standard for What Level of Drug Is Considered to Cause Intoxication Other Than Loss of the Normal Use of Mental or Physical Faculties**

There is no standard for what is intoxicating with drugs other than one's loss of the normal use of their mental or physical faculties. The Texas legislature has defined the legally intoxicating level for alcohol as0.08 or higher. Drugs do not have a baseline or standard number such as .08.

If the jury does not understand the lab report or what the state is alleging, or does not understand the toxicity levels, a wrongful conviction might result.

## How Do the Police Have Cause to Suspect Drug Use in a Driver?

We are often asked whether a police officer will automatically test for drugs in a person's system if the person has been drinking, or if the police officer has to specifically request a drug screening.

## The Type of Test Requested from a Driver Is Determined by the Police Office

In Bexar County, the police usually ask for a breath test first. We have had cases in which the breath test result was 0.0 and there was no odor of alcohol. But, the client was acting unusual. In these circumstances, the police officer can either apply for a blood warrant (if the client does not consent to a blood test) or have a DRE evaluation done.

## The Police Do Have Drug Recognition Expert (DRE) Officers on Their Force

There are officers who have specialized training to detect drug intoxication.  These officers are called drug recognition experts (DRE). A DRE uses his or her discretion to request specific tests based on their observations.

# WILL YOU BE CITED FOR A BREATH TEST RESULT BELOW THE LEGAL LIMIT OF 0.08?

We have handled cases in which the client blew below a 0.08 on a breath test and was still charged with DWI.

## Drivers Are Still Subject to Being Charged with DWI for a Breath Test Result below the Legal Limit

We have had some cases that were under the legal limit and were quickly dismissed by the State. We also had one case recently in which the State was aggressively seeking a conviction on a .06 breath test case. We started the trial but before the jury was brought in the State threw in the towel and dismissed the case.

## The Prosecutor Will Have Difficulty Proving This Type of Case

When the breath test is below the legal limit the prosecutor will difficulty proving the case. Let's say the breath test was just below the legal limit. A zealous prosecutor may try to argue to a jury that even though a person blew a 0.07 at the time of the breath test at 1:00 a.m., the suspect's blood alcohol was probably higher when they were stopped at 11:45 p.m.

In our opinion, these cases are usually not good cases for the State to take to trial. However, the law states that you are legally intoxicated if you have lost the normal use of your mental or physical faculties even if you have a blood alcohol lower than 0.08. The lesson to be learned is that even if your breath test result is under 0.08, you are not necessarily off the hook. You still need an attorney to help you try to beat the case.

## DOES TEXAS ALLOW ALTERNATIVE PUNISHMENTS FOR A DWI CONVICTION?

We have talked about convictions resulting in probation and/or jail time, but there are alternative punishments available in some situations.

## The Courts in Volk & McElroy, LLP's Area Do Not Offer a Diversion Program for First Offense DWI Charges

As of the writing of this book, in Bexar County, there is no such thing as any type of pre-trial diversion for a DWI charge. Pre-trial diversion is a great program that some Texas courts have in which they will give a first-time DWI offender a second chance by granting a dismissal if the offender complies with various requirements such as ignition interlock, wearing an ankle monitor, or other similar restrictions.

Unfortunately for Bexar County residents, the District Attorney's office here has a no-drop policy and does not offer a pre-trial diversion program for DWI offenses.

## An Alternative Punishment Such as an Ankle Monitor Still Equates to a Conviction

That being said, you sometimes can be given an ankle monitor or some of these alternative punishments in lieu of probation or jail time. There are a limited amount of clients that find this option useful.

## In Volk & McElroy, LLP's Area, Many First Offenders Receive Probation Upon Conviction

A first-time offender who presents himself well to the Court and does not show a brazen disregard for the community will generally receive probation without jail time if he or she is convicted after losing their jury trial. This is not a bright line rule. A first time offender can receive jail time as punishment or a condition of probation depending on the facts of the case or their criminal history. You should take your case very seriously and follow the advice of your attorney to try and avoid any potential jail time.

## SHOULD YOU RETAIN AN ATTORNEY FOR A DWI CASE? IN EVERY CASE, THE RIGHT ATTORNEY CAN MINIMIZE THE EFFECTS AND CONSEQUENCES OF A DWI CHARGE FOR HIS OR HER CLIENTS

A skilled DWI lawyer will always attempt to minimize the aggravation, punishment, and financial consequences a person is facing. We have been successful on a variety of

cases as a result of a jury delivering a NOT GUILTY or the Court throwing the case out.

Even in cases where we lose, we still do everything within our power to present our client in a light favorable to the Court. We believe that the punishment has to fit the crime and the person accused of it.

We had a 21-year-old dental student who was a first-time DWI offender where the plea bargain offer was very heavy-handed. The "bargain" included up to two years probation with ten days in jail, and a $1,200 fine. We tried the case and we lost it even though we put on a great defense. Because we presented our client in a favorable light, he was sentenced to a very manageable probation that was nine months long with no jail time. Sadly, he passed away a few months after completing probation. As lawyers we do everything we can to help our clients pick up the pieces after their arrest. Ultimately life is short and our job is to help improve the quality of your life to the best of our ability.

### In Every Case, the Judge Should See the Attorney's Client in the Best Possible Light

The Judge, when determining a sentence, must look at the individual, the case, and how it was resolved. Was it a plea bargain? Was it a jury trial? We have found that judges get to know defendants and clients through the jury trial process, and we have been lucky enough to have some of the best clients. Our clients present themselves well, they speak well, they have families, they own businesses, and they live productive lives. That has an influence on how the case is ultimately decided.

In every case, whether we win, lose, or plea bargain, as experienced DWI attorneys, we will fight to get the best result possible.

## CAN YOU AFFORD TO RETAIN AN ATTORNEY OR CAN YOU AFFORD NOT TO RETAIN AN ATTORNEY FOR A DWI CASE?

The cost of a DWI defense can vary widely from attorney to attorney. Defending a DWI case does have costs. Besides attorney's fees you could be faced with court costs, driver's license fees, probation fees, increased automobile insurance premiums, and lost time for work. The financial hardship may be worsened if you lose your job from a DWI conviction.

## A DWI Conviction Has Major Financial Consequences

DWI convictions have major financial consequences. If you hire an attorney and your case is dismissed or you are acquitted, you can save yourself a lot of money, aggravation, and your good name.

## Hiring an Experienced Attorney to Defend a DWI Case Is a Prudent Investment; Many Consequences of a Conviction Are Not Negotiable

Hiring a competent DWI attorney is the best investment you can make when facing these problems because the penalties are severe if you are convicted. Most of them are not negotiable, especially when it comes to your career.

Hiring an attorney could save you money in the long run. The actual cost of hiring an attorney depends on many factors including the attorney's experience and the type of DWI case. For example, the attorney's fees for a DWI 6th will be higher than a DWI 1st.

Our law office charges reasonable fees and offers a free consultation. We want to help you fight your DWI.

## IS IT DIFFICULT TO MOVE ON WITH YOUR LIFE FOLLOWING A DWI?

People can do many things once their case is over in order to get their life back on track.

### If Your DWI Case Is Acquitted or Dismissed, Your Record Can Be Expunged

If we win your case in trial or if your case is dismissed, you will be eligible for an expunction of criminal records.

Expunging those records and having them destroyed is usually the final step for a client to really put this behind them after a win.

## Volk & McElroy, LLP's Advice: Fulfill Any Requirements and Avoid a New Arrest

People who lose their case unfortunately can never have the arrest or criminal records expunged. For people who are convicted, our advice to them is this: complete probation promptly with no problems, make sure you fulfill all the requirements. Once you have completed probation, do not get arrested again for anything because you can face issues with escalating penalties.

We have had clients for whom we lost the case and we run into them, and they say, "I'm doing fine. I haven't had any problems since then. I completed probation, and I'm working, and I appreciate everything you did for me."

## Volk & McElroy, LLP's Clients Are Encouraged to Stay in Touch with the Firm

We hear from a lot of our former clients regularly, whether we won their case or not. We tell clients, at the end of the representation, "If you need anything call us, even if it is just a legal question that we may or may not be able to help you with, call me first. If I cannot help you, I will direct you to someone who can." That is how we do things here, and most lawyers who care about their clients do that as well.

## IT BEARS REPEATING: THERE IS A VIABLE DEFENSE FOR EVERY CASE

We have one last bit of advice for those arrested for DWI in Texas.

You **can win** your case. Hope is not lost. You are not doomed. Every case is different and we cannot make a general guarantee of winning any case (no attorney can). However, if you are arrested, you can hire an attorney who is experienced in DWI defense to advise you.

You will be amazed at the results an attorney who is experienced can produce for you.

The police are out there looking to make DWI arrests. You should do everything you can to avoid getting behind the wheel if you have been drinking. But, if something happens, call us to defend you.

## Volk & McElroy, LLP Offers a Free Consultation

Our address is 3003 NW Loop 410, Suite 100, San Antonio, Texas, 78230.

Our phone number is 210-377-1414.

You can call us 24/7. Our staff will answer or you can leave a message; we will return your call.

Our DWI website is www.winmydwi.com. We offer a free consultation. If you or a loved one has been arrested, let us help you. The best thing to do is to call us directly to set up an appointment. Whether we represent you or not, use this book to answer some questions you may have or to help you find an attorney that's right for you.

## DISCLAIMER:

This publication is informational only. No legal advice is being given, and reading this material creates no attorney-client relationship. If you are facing legal issues, whether criminal or civil, seek professional legal counsel to have your questions answered.

**Volk & McElroy, LLP**
3003 NW Loop 410, Suite 100
San Antonio, TX 78230
(210) 377-1414
www.WinMyDWI.com